# Reflections on STARTING STRONG

T0071164

## A New Teacher's Journal

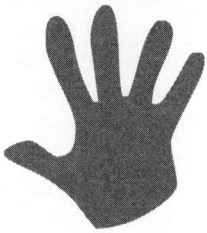

Skyhorse Publishing

Copyright © 2004 by Pearson Education, Inc.
First Skyhorse Publishing edition 2015

All rights reserved. No part of this book may be reproduced in any manner without the express written consent of the publisher, except in the case of brief excerpts in critical reviews or articles. All inquiries should be addressed to Skyhorse Publishing, 307 West 36th Street, 11th Floor, New York, NY 10018.

Skyhorse Publishing books may be purchased in bulk at special discounts for sales promotion, corporate gifts, fund-raising, or educational purposes. Special editions can also be created to specifications. For details, contact the Special Sales Department, Skyhorse Publishing, 307 West 36th Street, 11th Floor, New York, NY 10018 or info@skyhorsepublishing.com.

Skyhorse® and Skyhorse Publishing® are registered trademarks of Skyhorse Publishing, Inc.®, a Delaware corporation.

Visit our website at www.skyhorsepublishing.com.

10 9 8 7 6 5 4 3 2 1

Library of Congress Cataloging-in-Publication Data is available on file.

Cover design by Pearson Education, Inc.

Print ISBN: 978-1-62914-722-2
Ebook ISBN: 978-1-63220-105-8

Printed in the United States of America

**Whatever you can do,**
**or believe you can,**
**begin it.**
**Boldness has genius,**
**power and magic in it.**

—JOHANN WOLFGANG VON GOETHE

**If your plan is for one year, plant rice;**
**If your plan is for ten years, plant trees;**
**If your plan is for a hundred years,**
**Educate children.**

—CONFUCIUS

**Nothing great was ever achieved without enthusiasm.**

—RALPH WALDO EMERSON

**Better than a thousand days of diligent study is one day with a great teacher.**

—JAPANESE PROVERB

The whole art of teaching is only the art of awakening the natural curiosity of young minds for the purpose of satisfying it afterwards.

—ANATOLE FRANCE

**It is today that we create the world of the future.**

—ELEANOR ROOSEVELT

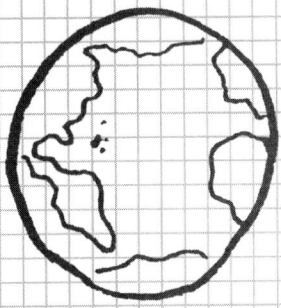

**Education is not preparation for life; education is life itself.**

—JOHN DEWEY

**Education is not the filling of a pail, but the lighting of a fire.**

—W. B. YEATS

**It is the supreme art of the teacher to awaken joy in creative expression and knowledge.**

—ALBERT EINSTEIN

**Instruction begins when you, the teacher, learn from the learner; put yourself in his place so that you may understand . . . what he learns and the way he understands it.**

—SOREN KIERKEGAARD

**A vision without a task is a dream.**
**A task without a vision is drudgery.**
**But a task with vision can change the world.**

—BLACK ELK

**A teacher affects eternity; he can never tell where his influence stops.**

—HENRY B. ADAMS

**The teacher is one who made two ideas grow where only one grew before.**

—ELBERT HUBBARD

**To raise new questions, new problems, to regard old problems from a new angle requires creative imagination and makes real advances.**

—ALBERT EINSTEIN

**Education is the key to unlock the golden door of freedom.**

—GEORGE WASHINGTON CARVER

**The secret of education lies in respecting the pupil.**

—RALPH WALDO EMERSON

**Every job is a self-portrait of the person who did it.**
**Autograph your work with excellence.**

—UNKNOWN